Be Eccentrich Inc & The Def Poet's Society Presents
WRITTEN BY JONKEL
BREAKDOWNS BY NICK FURY
TRAUMA MONSTERS:
THE BREAKDOWNS
Because you won't get it until you get it.

Trauma Monsters: The Breakdowns

JonKeL

Published by JonKeL, 2024.

TRAUMA MONSTERS: THE BREAKDOWNS

First edition. March 4, 2024.

Copyright © 2024 JonKeL.

ISBN: 979-8224807383

Written by JonKeL.

This is dedicated to writers of all walks. Poets, rappers, playwrights, songwriters, authors and everyone in between. We are all family in this field. We are all PenHedz and we can't be stopped.

Introduction

Spoken word, or performance poetry, is an art form that combines poetry and theater. Unlike "page poetry" spoken word has the sole purpose of being performed on a stage in front of an audience. It's no coincidence that I fell in love with poetry and theater at the same time, which might explain my unique style.

In this book I chose a small selection of poems from *Trauma Monsters: A Collection of Poetry* to be "broken down" and analyzed. I decided to collaborate with Nick Fury (@nickfurythepoet) when I discovered his uncanny ability to dissect words to uncover what's hidden. His writing style is very intricate, so I knew he could take on this project even when he was unsure of himself. He was able to expose parts of my work that opened other emotional doors. I mean, I actually cried after reading how he interpreted my pieces. So that let me know, the healing process isn't over. **(Side note: Poets if you've never had your work broken down in this way I highly recommend it. It will change the way you view your craft.)**

I hope this book can be used as a tool to help people understand the nuances that make up poetry. If you ever wanted to write in this style or explore other forms of creative expression, this is a great place to start. Educators and teaching artists, this is for you. New poets and old heads, this is for you. Those looking for another way to heal from and process trauma, this is for you. As an added bonus, I've included 6 brand new pieces from my next book, *The Art of the First Draft.*

Trauma Monsters

*1

I've never been a big fan of horror movies.
I don't think that they're bad,
they just don't scare me
the way real life has.

• Jonkel starts this poem off with a "set up" line designed to set the tone. By referencing horror movies, he's planting a seed that will continue to grow until the end of the poem.

*2

I don't believe in stories about the Candyman.
Out of fear I'd never say my trauma's name
5 times in a mirror.

• Candyman is a film franchise started in '92. The plot of the movie spoke of an urban legend of a lynched slave & artist would come take vengeance on those who spoke his name 5 times in a mirror. This reference is both straightforward, but leaves room for interpretation as well. Is he referencing generational traumas too?

*3

Serial slashers can't cut me
any deeper than I've sliced myself.

• Slasher is a double entendre and call back. Slasher is a style of horror film known for serial killers who use blades or knives. This calls back to *1 about how his real life is scarier than the movies to the point of self harm.

*4
I've seen death
enough times to know
it doesn't always appear in the shadows,
wearing a hood.
In my hood the masked men
weren't always the killers to run from.

● This section is meant to set up the next few stanzas. He is telling you he's familiar enough with death that he knows it has many faces. The hooded men he'd been taught to be scared of weren't the only threats he had to be aware of. Sometimes, the ones who are supposed to protect you are the ones who do the bidding.

*5
Sometimes the **b**utchers wore **b**lue.
Blue as the face of my mother
gasping for **b**reath

● Subtle use of alliteration (*see highlighted) adds a sense of syncopated rhythm.

*6
under the knee of that cop.
He must've been a vampire
the way he sucked the life out of her future.

● This is the first call back to section *4. A person in the role of a protector causing harm. Calling the police officer a vampire and referencing a monster keeps the horror metaphor in motion. This is the beginning to a list of different "trauma monsters" the poet has experienced.

*7
The past made my mummy dead inside.
Wrapped up her war wounds

● Having the life sucked out of her, his mom became a "mummy wrapped in war wounds". This takes the cliche popsicle stick dad joke pun of mommy/mummy and adds a new layer with an unexpected twist.

*8
Only to pass down that pain
through poor parenting.
But you can't blame the monster
for what Frankenstein
I mean Reagan did.

● The state of his mother and the condition of his neighborhood both create their own generational traumas. Living in the Black Community in the 80's during the crack epidemic and the subsequent war on drugs turned many people into "Frankenstein's Monster"

*9
Crack in the 80s
Turned my block into Elm Street.
A nightmare filled with the walking dead.
5 dollar head and 5 dollar hits
Was never enough to keep them fed.
Those Crack zombies ate my family alive.

● Nightmare on Elm Street reference illustrates the horror of seeing your community looking like it was taken over by Zombies. The Walking Dead TV show reference brings to life the imagery of the people left ravaged. Entire neighborhoods and households were devoured and this is all being witnessed when the poet was less than 10 years old.

*10
I couldn't do anything except hide
under the covers
when my uncle crept in my room.
It must've been the full moon
that brought the beast out of him.
That night I learned that addiction
can make the boogeyman hide under your bed.
Wait for you to fall asleep
and steal everything including your dreams.

● This section is another call back to section *4. The full moon turned his Uncle into a Werewolf. The implications of sexual abuse are explicit yet the author doesn't come out and say what happened. Instead he uses metaphor as a vehicle to carry on the theme of failed protectors turned boogeyman.

*11
I don't need to replay my trauma
on the big screen.
Stephen King couldn't write these stories.
The sematary in my city
was filled with pets and my best friends.

● This section is a call back to the first line of the poem. This time the author challenges even one of the greatest horror writers of all time in Stephen King couldn't write these stories. He reinforces this by referencing King's Pet Semmetary juxtaposed against the friends he'd lost.

*12
Where the loudest bumps in the night
came from the gunshots.
The sound of the chi chi chi cha cha
chopper makes every heart stop.

● Bumps in the night is a reference to kids stop motion show from the mid 90's, as well as a colloquial saying meaning the sounds the ghost makes; those unexplainable noises you hear at night. Jonkel expertly reinforces his primary theme again by comparing those noises to the sounds of gunshots. The next line creates a reference to Friday the 13th's iconic theme music before subverting expectations and smoothly creating a punchline.

*13
There's something striking about suspense.
The way it builds up,
leaves your audience hanging
from a rope.
Or on the edge of their seats.
Before my story reaches its climax.

● The author creates a sense of suspense, while building up to the poem's climax. This is very meta, referencing the themes within the themes horror.

*14
I fight back.
Armed with poetic silver bullets,
words whittled into wooden stakes, and a chest plate
forged from freedom.

I refuse to be another black character
that dies in the first scene.
No matter what the critics say.
I won't let my art imitate life.

● This section references the common weapons used against monsters, showing the arsenal the author has built up in response to his upbringing. A subtle use of both W & F alliteration creates a flow that mimics a climatic scene. Ending with a survivors mentality and refusal to let his life be predetermined, to follow the script. He's writing his own story regardless of the critics.

Hip Hop Check Up

*1

Congratulations Hip Hop Turning 50 is a BIG deal
Baby, Baby!
But if you're not Ready to Die

• It's appropriate the author starts with an ode to Biggie
Smalls adlib "Baby, Baby". This adlib is most notably on one
of Biggie's biggest hits "Juicy" off his album Ready to Die. It's
appropriate we started with the King of New York because if
alive today he too would be 50.

*2

I suggest you take better care of yourself or else,
Your album won't be the only one to get shelved.
There's so many ways to improve your health.

• The author creates themes early on starting with the title
"Hip Hop Check Up". His perspective is almost one of a long
time family doctor and friend. There is a personal stake in it
for the narrator.

*3

First of all, You should consider anger management.
Because you've been beating and bruising women till they turned
Blueface
Slapped them around on the windiest days like Breezy
Still don't believe me?
Ask D. Barnes and Michel'le
Who got the original Beats by Dre.

• This section sounds like the disappointed friend or family member bringing up all of Hip Hop's old dirt. Referencing several instances involving artist allegedly assaulting various female victims from modern day like Blueface, an older reference to Chris Brown and Rihanna, and finally taking it back to the early 90's creating a double entendre for "Beats by Dre"

*4
Hurt people hurt people
But that doesn't make it okay.
With all that you've been through
Your mental health has to be compromised.

• This section again conveys the disappointment of someone who deeply cares but is conflicted with their affections. Knowing that in loving this music, you are associating yourself with all its baggage as well.

*5
With All Eyez On You,
You survived a coastal war

• All Eyez on You (Me) is a reference to the Tupac album was the last album released during the prolific artist career; a career cut short due to the East vs West coast beef with the aforementioned Notorious B.I.G

*6
Suffered Heartbreaks in this Dark Twisted Fantasy,
Got Rich and almost Died Trying

• Heartbreaks & Dark Twisted Fantasy are referring to Kanye's albums. Kanye's 808's & Heartbreak was a project made as Kanye coped with the loss of his mother and longtime girlfriend. This dark time in his life was followed by one of his best projects, My Beautiful Dark Twisted Fantasy. Interestingly the author pairs the Kanye reference to an early skeptic of his, 50 cent, in the next bar. Get Rich or Die Tryin was 50's debut album.

*7

But yesterday's price is not today's.
Didn't you know, it's bad luck to step on the crack, Joe.
Your arteries have been Locked Up
So much,
They've arrested your cardiac.
The Fat Boys are just a Big Pun
For a heart attack.

● This section Jonkel really steps up the wordplay, continuing to blend references between health and hip hop. "Crack, Joe" is a subtle reference to Fat Joe aka Joey Crack. "Locked up so much, they arrested your cardiac" isn't just a clever play on words, it's also a set up between the Fat Joe line and the next line. As their names imply, Joe and Pun were hefty individuals. They were a part of the same record label and were close friends. The author then references another legendary rap group in the Fat Boys to drive home the comparison. What really makes these lines hit is the sad passing of Big Pun to an actual heart attack.

*8

Gluttony is still a deadly sin.
Time to get your cholesterol in check,
Beef can't be your only cash cow.

• These couple of lines are transition lines connecting the authors next points. In continuing the theme from the last section, Jonkel drives home the sad loss of Pun with "Gluttony is still a deadly sin". The theme of rappers dying continues, but the loss isn't about physical health anymore. It transitions with the line referring to "Beef". Not only something eaten, but also a slang term for a feud between one or more groups. Something hip hop was able to monetize very well as far back as Biggie and Tupac.

*9
No matter how wet your neck gets,
Young Dolphins can't outswim
100 shots.
So Drip or Drown
Sometimes Paper Routes
Lead to Dead Ends.

• This next section is an ode to Young Dolph who was tragically killed. Dolph was known for aggressive songs like "100 Shots". The author plays on the slang of diamonds being called "drip" with his references to water like "how wet your neck gets". Wrapping up the metaphor with the warning to "drip or drown". This is followed up with a reference to Dolph's record label Paper Route Empire. The author flips this metaphor with the punchline that the routes all lead to "dead ends".

*10
Your dietary intake could take your life.
You've been FED too much lead.
PnB got Rocked for eating chicken and waffles.
This ain't no Drill

Maybe you should lay off the Pop
Or get Smoked.

• Continuing the health awareness themes established earlier, Jonkel compares the force feeding of violent lyrics to PnB getting shot outside Roscoe's chicken in waffles. FED in this instance is also a double entendre for federal government agencies. He drives the point home by saying "this ain't no drill". Drill Rap was popularized in Chicago but has come under much criticism for its extremely violent lyrics. This is emphasized again by the death of Drill rapper Pop Smoke.

*11
Be careful what fuels your rocket.
You might Take Off and never return.
Houston ain't the only place with problems.

• Again the author warns hip hop to move with caution using some clever wordplay referencing the death of Migos rapper Takeoff, who was killed in Houston. This is all set up with the line "careful what fuels your rocket".

*12
I wonder how many Hip Hop heroes are in heaven?
Because Jesus Walks with
Street Disciples.
But Sunday Service isn't your only salvation.

• The author wonders about all the MC's lost to violence that are now in heaven while referencing Kanye's song "Jesus Walks" and him hosting "Sunday Service", as well as God's Son rapper Nas's album "Street Disciples".

*13

Therapy plus theology will bring you a real revelation.
And I know it feels like
You got nothing to lose it's just,
You Against the World.
And ain't it a Cole World?

● The author offers Hip Hop some more advice by saying therapy can coincide with spiritual beliefs for better healing. "You (Me) against the World" illustrates the feeling many disenfranchised youth feel when growing up in adversity. Something Hip Hop has done since the beginning. This point is driven home by the "cold world" cliche. The author again injects famous album names by Tupac, as well as J. Cole's album with similar themes "Cole World".

*14
Because they keep pushing,
Knowing how close you are to the edge.
Made you walk around barefoot,
With all that broken glass everywhere.

● The next few lines are all references to lyrics from the iconic song "The Message" by GrandMaster Flash and the Furious Five.

*15
But to be a Top Dawg means to balance between being the
Pimp and the Butterfly

● Jonkel warns in order to be the Top Dawd (Kendrick Lamar's label) you have to balance between being the "Pimp and the Butterfly" (One of Kendricks Albums).

*16

Your Levels of masculinity have become too toxic.
It's time for you to press pause
And stop it.
What will the Next 50 Years of your life look like?

● He uses this section to tie the end of the poem back to
the original premise of Hip Hop turning 50. Continuing the
theme of a concerned friend.

*17
Because you won't be a Lil' Baby forever
You ain't a Young Buck or Thug
That Double cup made you a Lil' Weezy
Don't let the Juice ruin your World
Remember even a Lil' Xan
Can turn OD, B

● Jonkel reminds hip hop how olds it's gotten, telling it it's
no longer a Young Buck (former G-Unit Rapper). He reminds
hip hop how the drug use caught up to it, all the
promethazine (double cup) made them sick (Lil Wayne aka
Lil Weezy has had a long documented issue with drinking
lean). This is further emphasized by the reference to rapper Lil
Xan, who battled with addiction to Xanax. The author uses
some clever phonetics to play on the term OD, and the slang
term "B". Together this references the early death of Wu Tang
member ODB.

*18
Your masters made you Grand
But your life can be over in a Flash.
This is The Message.

● Masters refers to the master tracks that are owned and generates money from royalties. This is also a call back to GrandMaster Flash's The Message.

*19
Love Yourself or Lose Yourself,
You only get
One Shot.

● He ends with a reference to Eminem's Oscar winning song Lose Yourself from the movie 8 Mile. In the intro the rapper refers to this being his "One Shot".

Zero to 60
Synopsis:

This poem brings the theme of fast cars to life using a multitude of poetic devices; however my favorite may be the way the author builds and releases tension. It's very much like riding passenger experiencing the slight lull of the engine before the gears re-engage throwing you back in your seat. This poem not only explores the extended metaphor of "fast cars", it takes you on a ride in one.

*1
Super cars possess a different level of power.
I'm talking 11 hundred pounds of torque.
15 hundred horsepower,
with a max speed of 200+ miles per hour.
Do you know what zero to 60
in 2.3 seconds feels like?
It feels like seeing your best friend,
at the age of 7 get killed by a bus
after running to get a ball that you threw.
If only the bus hit the brakes as fast as my heart did.

● This initial setup is what is referred to as a tension builder. It leaves the audience/reader anticipating where the writer is going with this? The answer is as quick and unexpected as a car crash delivering a punchline that punches you in the gut. Finishing with a metaphor illustrating the feeling of your heart stopping as you watch your best friend get killed. This section is a fantastic Introduction to the poem and ends with a strong hook to grab attention.

*2

I was just a kid.
Growing up poor,
seeing my mom and dad getting high,
fighting over drugs.
Before Drake they went from zero to a hundred
so quickly that it ended in blood.

• This section is the beginning of the movie after the opening
credits. The author has established an early childhood story of
trauma in the introduction and is using this section to set the
scene for much of the upcoming stanzas. Illustrating how with
abusive addicts for parents known for quickly escalating, his
homelife was a "wreck" too.

*3
I learned how to move through life,
just as fast as those jackboys
running a hundred yard dash
through my grandma's backyard.
I always wondered who those empty purses
belonged to and if they lived.

• Here the author continues to establish his background and
how it relates to his upbringing. Watching purse snatchers
jumping fences to evade police left a young boy wondering if
those jack boys that looked so much like him were murderers.
Those were the role models he learned from.

*4
I lived in the fast lane
ever since I was given my last name.
I was so young,
my feet couldn't even reach the pedals.

How was I supposed to overcome
those hurdles with legs
as short as black life expectancy?
They never expected to see me
make it past 21.

● Jonkel starts to question the fast life even at a young age. Wondering how his short legs would allow him to jump similar fences/ hurdles; especially considering his life expectancy was nearing its expiration date. Subtle use of rhyme starts to create an additional layer of cadence that starts to subtly build tension again.

*5
Saying I grew up fast is an understatement.
When I spent most of my life
racing against adversities chasing freedom.
Running over any traces left of my innocence.

● Up to this point rhyme has been used infrequently. In this stanza the poet uses the multi syllable slant rhyme sounds of "A" and "N". Statement, racing, chasing, and traces creates a syncopated rhythm. The stanza ends in a culmination of wordplay ending in the punchline of "running over" his "innocence".

*6
I was forced to become a man
before I was shipped off at 17
and Sam became my uncle.
Before I could say my vote didn't count.

• After establishing the chaos of his childhood, the author shows how he was seeking answers to the previously posed questions by searching for stability in the armed forces before he was of legal age to vote.

*7
I was supposed to count
on my mother to teach me how to drive
and how to survive
the wilderness of this concrete jungle.
And since there's no church in the wild
then what's a mom to a non-believer.

• The author felt betrayed by a mother who didn't give him the driving lessons needed to navigate the roads he had to traverse in life. Jonkel references the Kanye Song "No Church in the Wild" as the punchline, while flipping the lyrics to subvert expectation. Searching for guidance in other places because he'd lost faith in the traditional routes.

*8
I always moved in top gear.
Anticipating the fear
of what was to come around the next corner.

• Top Gear is a reference to the British TV show of untrained celebrities attempting to drive different cars on race tracks and finish with the fastest times. Oftentimes the drivers would almost crash on tight corners. Corner in this usage is a double entendre for the life the writer was trying to race away from, hoping he doesn't crash in the same street corners as his peers.

This section is where the creativity of Jonkel really shows through. So far this story has started in the parking lot, pulled out onto the main drag and is at the stoplight before getting on the flat stretch of highway. As each gear shifts you can feel the tension build like riding passenger with someone driving their first car with a v8 engine. Each gear throws you back in your seat.

*9
1st gear!
While some of my friend's parents called
to invite their friends over for fight nights.
2nd gear!
My parents called
and invited the police over after knife fights.
To a child, domestic violence feels like war.

 • Creating a duality between his life and some of his friends, using a two syllable rhyme to hammer home the punchlines flipping Fight Night & Knife Fight. Using this as a setup to create a metaphor within the metaphor (very meta) comparing his upbringing to a warzone.

*10
3rd gear!
Walking around the house on eggshells.
Setting off land mines.
Dodging bullets and bombs.
I didn't need to play pretend
with little green army men.
I didn't need to go overseas
to oversee the damage that was done.

 • Continuing the war metaphor illustrates how his childhood made joining the military a natural progression.

*11
4th gear!
Dreams broken like limbs.
These battle scars may never heal.
Sometimes I pinched myself
to see if it was real and it was.
I never woke up from that nightmare.

• Even before he became a soldier, he knew that damage that had been inflicted was something he'd carry. When he writes "battle scars" he gives a subtle easter egg to his poem "Battle Poet", as well as a reference to his title poem "Trauma Monsters".

*12
5th gear!
I can still feel the tight grip
of depression's hands around my neck.
Taking away my breath,
choking me in my sleep.

• By 5th gear the build up is starting to crescendo. Using each gear to add another layer to the story and the background of the writer.

*13
6th gear!
Homeless by the age of 15
scraping up pennies for food to eat.
Stop!
I wish I could've just stopped.

● By the 6th gear you've been thrown back in your seat so many times before the author finally slams on the brakes. The "Stop!" gives you enough time to realize you were holding your breath, breaking the tension. Letting your heart rate slowly start to return to normal.

*14
But when traveling at the speed of light,
shooting stars don't die until they make impact.
And I'm hoping I don't burn out along the way.

● This stanza illustrates how helpless the author felt. The pace he's needed to keep up in life has made certain outcomes feel inevitable. This is also the first tone switch within the poem. After all the darkness in the story we finally see a glimmer of light. The very thing our main character was looking for all along. He gives us a couple more double entendres with "shooting stars" referring to up and coming celebrities in the limelight and "burn out" referring to stars and tires.

*15
There's still air in my tires.
My pistons are still pumping.
There's plenty of fuel left in my tank.
I've learned to control my need for speed
but I wasn't breaking the law.
I was just,
keeping up with the flow of traffic.

● Bringing us back to the fast cars metaphor to close the loop, Jonkel shows he hasn't lost hope. How he found a place in life where you don't always need to be red lining in order to survive. Finishing with a great closing line that draws the parallel between his life and those who grew up in similar conditions. To some he may have been living a fast life, to those in the know, he was just keeping up with traffic.

Battle Poet
Synopsis:

This is a slam poem. It is meant to be read in a competitive setting. From the 4th wall breaking introduction to the final lines this poem is a defiant challenge to any other poet who hears this battle cry. The author competes against other poets while simultaneously fighting with the monsters of his past. The primary imagery the poet creates, parallels the metaphor of "battle". Using this imagery to paint a picture of the complexity of his past.

*1
They call a poetry slam
a battle.
Except I've had my back against the ropes
in real life bouts.
These rounds here
ain't nothing for me to get through.
Nothing like the rounds that went through
my grandma's window
during those shootouts.

● Using poetry slam lingo in this introduction section creating double entendres around the words "bouts" and "rounds" comparing poetry to the fighting in a boxing match. Rounds actually becomes a triple entendre in the sixth line when he evolves to include bullet round as well.

*2
I've been at war since 7.
Witnessed too many soldiers
make their ascent to heaven.
Death seems to be

the only promise in life.

• Continuing the theme of battle, JonKel starts revealing his past to illustrate to the reader his familiarity with a violent life.

*3
You might
have seen me at an open mic
and thought, JonKeL be killin' that shit.
But you have no idea
how many wigs I had to split
to write like this.
How many beasts I slayed
to get on this stage.

• Talking directly to the audience the poet breaks the fourth wall. This section feels almost more like a battle rap than a poem. The poet introduces a more consistent rhyme scheme with: Might/ Mic, Shit/ Split/ This/, and Slayed/ Stage.

*4
Addiction had my family chasing dragons.
I swear I saw my uncle breathe fire
whenever he hit his crack pipe
under the moonlight.

• Chasing dragons refers to an addict (usually harder drugs like heroin, meth, crack, PCP) chasing a high that is as good as the first time. The author then flips this metaphor to an almost childlike perspective of his uncle breathing fire.

*5
Before bootcamp the war on drugs was my first deployment.
PTSD wasn't the only demon

that afflicted me.
I lost one of my childhood limbs
in close quarters combat.

● This section continues the battle metaphors comparing the PTSD of growing up during the war on drugs to his time in the military. He refers to losing a childhood limb. This is in reference to what happens to a child emotionally during violent situations; the feeling of losing a piece of yourself.

*6
I went hand to hand with my dad
while my mother was locked away in Mia.
Pieces of her still MIA
I, another POW.
No boy should know how it feels
to punch his pops.
I still have scars all over this purple heart.

● Piggy backing off the last line in the prior stanza JonKel talks about fighting his dad, which explains how he lost a "limb". First he uses Mia geographically to set the scene of South Florida, then referring to his mother as MIA, an acronym for Missing in Action. This designation was given to soldiers who were assumed dead or captured. He continues by calling himself a POW (Prisoner of War), another designation popularized during the wars in Vietnam and Korea. POW is also used in the poetic device onomatopoeia, creating a double entendre and really bringing to life the imagery of the next line. He finishes this stanza with a reference to the Purple Heart, a medal awarded to those who were wounded in combat tying the stanza together. Leaving us with another double entendre in "purple heart" being his bruised emotions.

*7
But what's a war-wound
to a battle poet?
A score of 30?
A dope ass bar?
Perhaps catharsis helps us get this far.
Because I never would have made it
without this slingshot of a pen.
My middle name is David,
so what better way
to take down poetic Goliaths
than to have them all flown in.
From Baltimore to LA
to Pompano and back again.

● After surviving the trials of his past, Jonkel takes this moment to show that his time growing up in a warzone had left him bulletproof. He brushes off the judgment of the crowd, the judges, and the Poet who inspired the piece, Black Chakra from Baltimore. Chakra has such a presence in the poetry community, he stands like a Goliath. JonKel highlights this by comparing his pen to a slingshot, while giving us his real middle name David.

*8
Warriors of different disciplines
compete in this here bloodsport.
Van Damme you,
if you thought we just came to kick it.

● Comparing poetry slams and the many different styles of spoken word, to the disciplines of martial arts tournaments. The movie Bloodsport launched the career of Jean-Claude

Van Damme and his impressive kicking style into stardom. So even though poets are a tight knit community, when it comes to slam, we're coming for your head.

*9
Yeah we Sly and the Family Stone
until explosive words get thrown.
I really have pulled a grenade pin before.

● Referencing Sly and the Family Stone's breakup from volatile words being thrown about, the poet reminds us that pulling a grenade pin is nothing new.

*10
Call me the assassin with compassion.
I hate leaving bodies on the floor.
I'm sorry but my mamma said
knock y'all out.
Pound for pound.
I stood toe to toe with the best around.
And yeah my record ain't perfect.
I took some losses over the years.

● He follows up with stanza continuing the theme of the duality of poetry slams. Though he feels compassion for the other poets, it's still a fight. Never forgetting his love for hip hop, he references LL Cool J's *Mama Said Knock You Out*, and while using fight lingo such as Pound for Pound (a ranking system for the best fighters regardless of weight class) he admits he's taken some losses from some great champions.

*11
One thing I do know,

is that I don't have many fears.
So how can I be afraid of a poet?
When I was never afraid
of an eviction notice.
Life's left hook hits harder
when you're homeless.
I went 12 whole rounds
with that heavyweight.

• Despite those losses, he's learned to not fear these great champions. He's taken too many hard hits (left hooks) in life to worry about getting a low score. He's gone into deep waters with heavyweights (12 rounds is a full boxing match) when others would've been knocked out.

*12
I've jumped out of frying pans,
into so many fires,
I even got burnt below the belt a few times.
But I never let that blacken my chakra.
I am the black boy
built by the backlash of battle.
Basted braised and broiled but
I ain't done cooking yet.

• Out of the frying pan and into the fire is a common saying for going from one bad situation to the next. This sets up a series of cooking related metaphors highlighted by the punchline "I ain't done cooking yet". There is also a subtle reference to Black Chakra amidst the rhythmic "B" alliteration.

*13

So if this is what they call a battle,
then the victory is already mine.
God gave me my 10s.
I don't need your 9s.

● Finishing the poem with a couplet, the poet is able to create a quick synopsis of the poem in just two lines. Referring to the 1-10 point system used in Slam, the poet ends with a defiant battle cry to the judges. Knowing at the end of the day their scores are irrelevant. Afterall, to this poet, what's another battle?

Bag Man

Synopsis:

This poem's primary theme is emotional baggage. We all weigh ourselves down by collecting burdens that over time will inevitably break us or we learn to put them down. JonKel explores this theme through the lens of Erykah Badu's "Bag Lady". If you're not familiar, please take a moment to listen before continuing. Don't worry, I'll wait. This poem is written almost as a response to "Bag Lady", using the metaphor Badu created and expanding upon the idea.

*1
Hey bag man, you gone hurt your back.
Dragging all them bags like that.
I guess nobody ever told you,
That all you must hold onto is you.
Can someone please tell the woman
by the window seat,
that the bag man's back aches too.
And if you don't learn to bend with the knees,
your back might break too.
This weight ain't easy y'all.

● The intro starts like Badu's with near matching lyrics. While Erykah's perspective focuses on the bags women carry, JonKel uses this as a set up to flip it and use it as a catalyst for the struggle men go through as well.

*2
I've been chasing bags
while carrying these bags since birth.
Inherited a matching set from my father

because genetics be funny that way.
I remember going to school everyday
with a backpack full of fear.
Too afraid to shed a tear,
ain't have no room for emotions in there.
I had to save space for my blackness.
Overpacked it with so much pride,
that I could crouch down
and hide inside it's shadow.

• A central theme in Trauma Monsters is nature vs nurture. The author explores this theme again in the genetics he carries from his father. He shows subtle humor referring to his balls as a matching set of bags he inherited from his father. He carried this burden as a child does, in a backpack. Learning to stuff all the things inside both good and bad. He refers to hiding in its shadow. This implies he was hiding from the light of (insert belief system here), because even though the bags were a defense mechanism to survive, it also forced him to use it in ways that weren't healthy.

*3
The older I got the more bags I had to carry.
Buried myself underneath a facade of no good.
Stored my misogyny in a fanny pack,
kept it close to my manhood.
Thought I had a master key
to open any woman's heart.
Thought my flashlight
was the only way to see inside her dark,
until I got burnt sticking my candle in that wax.

● This stanza starts to explore the toll of weight carried. The poet uses an evolving metaphor to paint a series of pictures. His "key" to her "heart", "flashlight" to her "dark" left him burned out so to speak or did he catch an STD?

*4
My father wasn't around
to teach me how to act
so I taught myself how to handle this baggage.
Claimed I could avoid all that trouble
by stuffing everything inside of an Army duffle.
My mental health was broken in boot camp.
PTSD never felt more heavy.
So I packed it all up in a rucksack
and brought it back as a souvenir.

● Continuing the theme established in the previous stanza, the poet weaves in more of his story adding the weight of baggage he had accumulated over the years. Never learning how to put it all down, he continued by getting PTSD during his military service.

*5
Now I'm here carrying the bag of a husband.
Vowed in sickness and in health till death.
But I've been worried I'll come home
and find everything I own in a box to the left.
Momma said there'd be days like this.
Days when being faithful felt the hardest.
Nights when drunken texts
might not have been the smartest.
But I still think I know more than a 5th grader.
I don't know shit!

But I knew one day
all those bags would get in my way,
but I never once thought to pack light.

● As the story continues the poet explores how all this baggage affected his personal life and marriage. How the previously listed bad habits of misogyny still sometimes reared their ugly head. At this point in the story there is the implication of more maturity and growth since he's now married. This only sets up the pain and anger he feels at never "packing light".

*6
This load I've had to bear
has done nothing but prepare me for today.
Today I carry the diaper bag of a new father.
Confident though,
slightly bothered that I won't do better than him.
Fatherhood comes easiest to those
that want it the most.
And I want it badly.

● The narrative continues to shift to a more mature, and understanding version of our central character. Now a father, he's carrying a new kind of weight. The burden of responsibility he has wanted so badly.

*7
So this goes out to the bag man.
Never be afraid to ask for help.
Sometimes you have to loosen the straps,
unclinch your fits,
let it go, let it go, let it go, let it go.

And put down those bags for good.

- Bringing it back to "Bag Lady" the poet is able to give some advice from someone who'd been there; Put those bags down and let it go.

Invasion

Synopsis:

It is poems like this that bring to mind the quote "the pen is mightier than the sword". In the hands of a master, the pen can always cut much deeper. The beauty of metaphor is how you can take two different subjects and use the power of comparison to give a shift in perspective. This perspective can make all the difference in actually being able to change someone's viewpoint in a world of echo chambers. Jonkel is able to masterfully compare invading colonizers to an alien invasion. Drawing parallels over and over through clever wordplay and tongue in cheek humor. Jonkel is able to do all this while talking about an incredibly sensitive and important topic without losing sight of his message.

*1

Most people think I'm weird
because I believe in Aliens.
Some even call me crazy
when I say that I've seen them
with my own two eyes.
But I wasn't the first.
Stories of their explorations
have been depicted on cave walls,
painted by my ancestors.

• His initial setup is a bit coy, playing on the tropes of someone who has "seen" an alien. You can almost imagine him telling the tale in a hushed whisper of someone about to tell you all about their favorite conspiracy theory. Like a magician, this misdirection only adds to the reveal. However, unlike a magician looking for immediate reaction, Jonkel slowly starts sprinkling clues over the next few stanzas revealing the face of the alien from his story.

*2
These ETs have conquered many lands.
So cultural assimilation
is what they do best.
They came in from the west,
descending from their spaceships.
La Amistad and Duc du Maine.

• A common theme of this poem will be movie references. Our first example shows up as a reference to Steven Spielberg's "ET". This movie depicted a friendly alien similar to the first colonizers who came to trade, before the next wave came to make war. Another clue is given for our history nerds out there, name dropping notorious slave ships La Amistad and Duc Du Maine.

*3
Us natives had never seen such vile creatures.
A nation of snake people,
covered in human skin
attempting to blend in
to look like the masses.
The only way to see their true identity
is to view them through
special woke glasses.
Just like in the movies.

• Illustrating the confusion Africans must have felt at their pale invaders, the author references a conspiracy theory about an alien reptile species living amongst us (*look up Justin

Bieber is a reptile), as well as the Roddy Piper movie "They Live" in which Aliens have taken over the world but can only be seen when wearing a special pair of glasses.

*4
They Live amongst us,
beaming us up,
poking and prodding us with probes.
Alien abductions have a way of resembling
auction blocks.
They even cloned us to
create a race of beings in their own image.

● "They Live" becomes a double entendre from the previous setup. Continuing the theme of aliens and colonizing, stories of being probed and abducted become a lot more haunting when compared to slave auction blocks.

*5
Science fiction has a way of resembling
colonization.
Just like The Borg Collective
from Star Trek.
Their sole purpose
was to take other planets by force,
enslaving them.
All useful knowledge was retained for them.
While the irrelevant information
meaning our existence was erased.

● Using the similarities of Science Fiction and Colonization to illustrate one of the most difficult parts about being a descendent of the Slave Trade, is the obliteration of history.

Or the technologies lost to the ages because it wasn't deemed
useful to a culture who didn't understand its significance.
That's if it didn't end up in a Museum in France or Britain.

*6
But I don't expect you to believe
in life on other planets
or what you see on TV but trust me,
this is real.
Millions of lives have been
slaughtered and killed
in the name of their exploration.

● One of the most genius things about this poem is how
Jonkel is able to take such a heavy topic and keep the tone
light. In this section he brings back the conversational tone
used in section 1. This creates a break in the action, almost
dividing the poem into a second act. It's a brief slow down
before a barrage of wordplay.

*7
Planting phallic flags
and seeds inside soils
that were never meant for them.
Remember Will Smith taught us,
how to fight for our Independence Day
during times of Invasion.

● Using some slight alliteration, he ramps back up the pace.
Planting flags in soils becomes a double entendre for the rape
perpetrated by invading nations.

*8

Because when Mars Attacks,
these Predators will do more than just
Snatch your Bodies.
The Signs were all around us.
When standing on the Edge of Tomorrow

• Next comes a series of movie titles and references so quick
and witty you'll ask for a rewind. Independence Day kicks it
off, followed by Mars Attacks, Predator, Invasion of the Body
Snatchers, Signs, and Edge of Tomorrow.

*9
it can be hard to see them
lurking in the Skyline.
White tends to blend in
with the color of the clouds.
Bedsheets cloak their ghostly image.
Afraid to show us who they truly are
as if we'd understand
the complexities of their evil.
It's out of this world.

• Playing off the bedsheet ghost costume and its similarities
to the uniform of the KKK, the author is able to allude to an
other worldly evil.

*10
They've recently revealed themselves again.
January 6th they landed on Capitol Hill.
Dressed in khaki spacesuits,
white polo,
red helmet.
Thousands of them were marching,

shouting, "take us to our leader,
take us to the orange one!"
The War of the Worlds has begun again.

● The imagery used in this section brings back the tone of levity and playfulness. Using the old trope "take me to your leader" is comedy gold. This leads to another movie reference to War of the Worlds.

*11
Hard to tell who's foe or friend
when these Decepticons keep Transforming.
So save yourselves.
The Men In Black don't always come
when you need them most.

● The ending is the sign off with a couple more movie callbacks. The tone of which feels like a conspiracy theorist wrapping up his rant before saying goodbye. Leaving the reader wondering, what happens when the conspiracy is actually true?

Preview of "The Art of the First Draft"

There's something refreshing about reading a first draft. Knowing the creator could've spent more time editing the work, but chose to let it live as is. The perfection is found in the imperfections. Like listening to a jazz band during a jam session. The notes might be off, or the timing isn't perfect, but it's so beautiful. That kind of magic can only be found in the first draft.

Some of my favorite rappers have developed their skills so much that they no longer need to physically write. I adapted this technique and used it to craft my poetry. I started cultivating this skill due to my 4 hour long work commute. I would say a line and then keep adding to it until it was complete. When I got home, I'd brain dump it all and finish it that night. Creating in this way also helped me with memorization because I repeated those lines enough times that it actually sticks. This step isn't necessary, but it helps with audience engagement during a performance.

Enjoy these samples for now and look for the full project early 2025. As always, Thank You for your continued support.

Puppies Love

Puppy love is defined as

Intense but shallow romantic attachment associated with adolescents.

We were just puppies when we met.

And I was a little wild back then.

Still untamed,

sniffing around at every pooch that passed by.

Until you caught my eye.

I knew that you came from a different breed.

But I couldn't see what a healthy relationship looked like.

I didn't know what obedience meant.

I wasn't housebroken

because my house was broken.

My mother wasn't the best example of a lady

but my father was certainly a tramp.

Growing up in my doghouse wasn't a walk in the park.

Some days it was 4 of us to one dish.

Where wishbones were never evenly split.

But every moment spent with you put a wag in my tail that wasn't there.

You put a smile on my snout.

No matter what we talked about.

With ears perked at attention you would listen

to me howl at the moon,

when no one bothered to hear my bark.

Ever since I got down on my hind legs to beg for your paws in matrimony.

Forget man,

I'll always be your best friend.

Curl up and sleep right beside you,

Pray to Stay 20 toes down.
For your love in return
I'll do all the tricks.
Sit. Stay. Rollover.
As long as you rub my belly from time to time.
Scratch that itch I can't reach.
You know, let me bury the bone in that special place.
Put my face all in it when I'm drinking the water.
Because when you tell me to fetch,
I always bring back the wood.
And never get this misunderstood.
Love and loyalty is rarely seen in black and white.
So I try with all my might.
With every pound of pressure in my bite.
With every bit of grit in my growl.
I promise to hold you down
with the weight of a Great Dane.
Be your protector
and guard you like a German shepherd.
Lay on your lap for emotional support.
You rescued me and in the blink of an eye,
7 years has gone by
more than 3 times.
I've been in love so long
that after 20 something years my love is now fully grown.
And since this old dog is still learning new tricks,
What better gift can I give to my litter than love.

Heroes & Villains

As a youth mentor
  one of my favorite icebreakers is to ask a class,
  If they could be any superhero who would it be and why?
  One day a kid said he would be Antman.
  Because no bully would bother him if he stood as big as a building.
  That day after school
  I witnessed him confront his nemesis.
  I wanted to intervene
  but it wasn't my business.
  I felt powerless against a villain who's also his parent.
  Some origin stories must be written without edits.
  Being his professor,
  I just wanted to show him
  how to put an X on his negative thoughts.
  But as I watched Ant Man battle that Banshee,
  Her words struck him with such force that it forced him to use his
powers.
  Only this time,
  I saw him shrink to the size of nothing.
  Fear folded him into a different dimension.
  Her tongue split his atoms in half.
  And there he stood defeated, empty.
  The 15 year old shell of a young man left hollow.
  I could barely swallow.
  The iceman inside my eyes began to melt.
  I multiplied myself,
  so that both me and my inner child could speak up for him.
  I wanted to stretch out my arms and embrace him like a fantastic
father figure.
  But that thing,

attacked and rocked his world.
She was the human torch
That burned down his brilliance.
But ain't it strange how black boy magic only works in comic books.
What about the pain outside the pages?
How does he pass through those phases,
When his guardians couldn't guard his galaxy?
The universe is so bright but you can't marvel at a star's stolen shine.
She Thanosed his childhood away with just one snap.
Made him angry
just to put the weight of the world on his little hulk back.
Even in the multiverse,
a child and a provider cannot live in the same body.
If only I embodied the power of Jean Grey,
to make him forget for a bit.
And perhaps, like the phoenix
he can rise from the ashes,
she made of his dreams.
Her screams can't be the deafening of his future.
I'll be his Bishop,
And move these pieces of time,
In order to protect his present.
Past trauma
can be a punisher all by itself.
So I swoop down like
Silver Surfer,
and save his teen spirit.
His Nirvana will soon be in bloom.
I use my Chi
to give him the energy
to continue his fight.
Because None of us can do this on our own.

No hero in history ever has.
Not even your favorite.

See Through

I'm trying to be more transparent in my writing,
but no amount of windex seems to remove the streaks.
No offense to you housekeepers but this is what cleaning out your
closet looks like.
I'm showing you the aftermath,
all the shady parts.
That darkness is where the scary things go to hide.
Trauma is the hardest scar to hold inside.
It always has a way of seeping through the skin.
You can almost smell it in the air like pheromones.
Such a beautiful stench.
The fog of this funk makes it difficult to see my soul.
But you can't keep believing in those stories you were told.
How pitiful people punish with pain.
How the once hurt
now hurt folks.
This is me attempting to be crystal clear.
Even though I've been shattered.
Suffered so many cracks, it's no wonder why I couldn't be seen.
Oh lord, how stained my glass has gotten.
Yet somehow they only view the colorful hues.
Overlooking the smudges and the smears.
That spot appears,
whenever I think about the time
I stood over my father with a loaded gun.
He laid there sleeping so peacefully
and I just wanted to see him go out that way.
Because when he awakened,
I knew the war would soon follow.
His tongue was thick with manipulation.

I wondered if he was bulletproof?
Or Would he just break in two
and fall apart like our family did.
He hid, unseen behind the curtain.
Pulling all the strings to control my mother.
The persuasion of the puppeteer is powerful.
Perhaps Pinocchio was a prisoner.
When my mother was in prison,
I wasn't her son
I was her visitor.
When I put my hand in the ¼ inch thick acrylic,
Something about it distorted the vision.
I could see her,
But I couldn't see her.
And when she came home she was never the same.
Because some scratches never buff away.
Over time with enough sanding,
She was able to smooth out those scrapes.
Us poets construct these glass houses,
In front of audiences holding stones.
So I brace myself for an impact.
Hoping to make an impact.
Knowing a fracture is just a judgment away.
So I do it anyway.
I Strip myself of the coverings that keep me from breathing.
Bare my bones on this X-ray,
we call a stage.
Skeletons aren't made for closets,
Clothes are.
And when you're trying to be transparent,
Who needs them anyway.

Raid!

Where I'm from
      we were more afraid of cockroaches
      than gunfire.
      I know it sounds odd
      that I barely beat the odds.
      The only way I survived the gunshots was to crawl,
      Get down and lay low.
      Good thing we didn't have roaches on the floor,
      I would've really lost it.
      I could've lost my life when I saw one fly pass me.
      It came in through the window and hit the wall.
      And I didn't even flinch because bullets ain't scary like bugs.
      I know what it feels like to be feared.
      I've been called a black bug before.
      The exterminators in blue came thru the door
      Flashed their lights
      and watched us all scatter.
      Raid!
      And every time they sprayed
      I became a little more desensitized.
      The block was so hot
      that it felt like
      the Fourth of July
      But you didn't have to tell me
      how the fireworks
      Shots ring in the new year every other day
      a celebration
      in honor of another homicide.
      It's not until the invasion happens outside
      black neighborhoods,

that they care about fumigating.

Maybe we should start painting little roach wings on the backs of bullets, that would make people want to run.

My friend Jermaine Rolle couldn't outrun the big boot.

I lost him at the age of 9. His life ended too abrupt.

They stomped on him

and left him on his back belly up.

But that wasn't the last time I lost a friend to the trap.

That roach Motel

is the bait that keeps them coming back.

Fact, more people have picked up guns

Than have picked up bugs.

Some would prefer to drown out a hail of bullets,

Than to deal with a little water bug.

Something like this can't be covered up with a tent.

We've already been pumped with their poison.

Fed, lead to believe

That we need protection.

That the 2nd amendment will keep us safe.

I ask, who are the real enemies in the first place?

The gun owners or the manufacturers?

The lobbyists or the street jackers?

And yes we've been screaming,

stop the violence for a long time now and I don't know what else to do.

I just want you to imagine, an infestation of bullets crawling all over your neighborhood,

You would want to kill them too.

Juicing

I was thinking we try something different.

Something a little more healthy.

This recipe requires no meat at all. Because tonight I wanna eat it raw the vegetarian way.

So Put all the fruits and veggies on my plate.

My appetite for your appetizers can't wait.

Even though I was patient enough to make it through those mango seasons before I tasted your sweetness.

Your juice has always been my weakness.

When I nibble on your nectar

I use my tongue to search for your treasure.

Somewhere hidden behind a waterfall lies the most exotic passionfruit known to man.

Only This man.

It doesn't matter what you're dressed in

As long as you bring the dressing.

I'll be tossing salads like we'll be tossing clothes.

And no, you won't need that rose.

My watering mouth will be sure to keep your garden wet.

I bet, I know what them tulips need.

You already had this eggplant

but are you ready for my Johnny Appleseed.

Don't act like you ain't never been below bobbing for apples.

That up and down head motion.

All neck, no hands.

Girl you got the most fertile soil in all the lands.

Baby you can produce a harvest between your legs.

And I never been too proud to beg.

Plead, get down on my knees

and squeeze

Until you've been cold pressed.
Call this an organic orgasim.
I got that food for your soul
so be careful when feeding your face.
Because this,
artichoke you.
Only if you want to.
When I dig in it I get deeply rooted.
Call my lady an underground queen.
I mean, where do you think she get all them yams from?
Homegrown all natural with no GMOS.
DNA contains all the proof.
Everybody knows,
the blacker the berry
the sweeter the juice.
Antioxidants seeping from your skin.
Man Melanin and melons is more than a mouthful.
Mmm mmm mmm your body is poetic and I love alliteration.
But not more than I love your delicious detox.
Some diets change daily
but this love is a lifestyle,
That will last a lifetime.
As long as flowers are in bloom
And grass is green.
God gave us this gift of pleasure.
So we might as well
be fruitful.

Bad Boys

Bad boys are born every day
but they can't stop and won't stop the abuse.
Whether they kill you
or make you feel like you're ready to die,
the scars they leave can't always be seen with the naked eye.
It takes a certain flavor in the ear to hear what's really being said.
He said he would never hurt you
but he trapped you and gave you no way out.
Said he would only use his hands to wave them in the air like he
didn't care.
But he didn't care
because he used them to scratch, mix and rearrange your face.
She never thought a guy from Harlem would make her shake.
He said that he would change
but kept remixing the original version.
So many victims sing sad songs
but these are just some samples.
A few snippets from the soundtrack.
You know,
something to groom to.
Imagine a narcissist who can't stand his own reflection.
That kind of monster
must be a bloodsucker.
The music industry is already full of bloodshed.
All these bad boys are enough to keep the carpets red.
No amount of shiny suits
will ever hide the truth.
Because dance moves
only work on camera,
not in courtrooms.

And a name change might reinvent you but,
What's in a name?
That which we call a turd by any other word would smell just as
shitty.
It doesn't matter if we use birth names like Sean
Or nicknames like Diddy.
The voice of the victims must be amplified.
Look how easy it is for a manipulator to mute your microphone.
To engineer every edit,
Until you no longer recognize your own recordings.
Dollar signs can be distorting.
Being blinded by the bucks,
Can make a lot of us look the other way.
But I'm here to say,
we don't have to take that.
So take that!
We won't be silenced by the singles.
Radio isn't the religion I worship.
My body doesn't bop to those beats.
That rhythm no longer moves me.
But you do you.
You have the freedom to listen to whatever you want to.
So go ahead and press play
but remember,
It won't pause the pain.
It only keeps the record spinning.

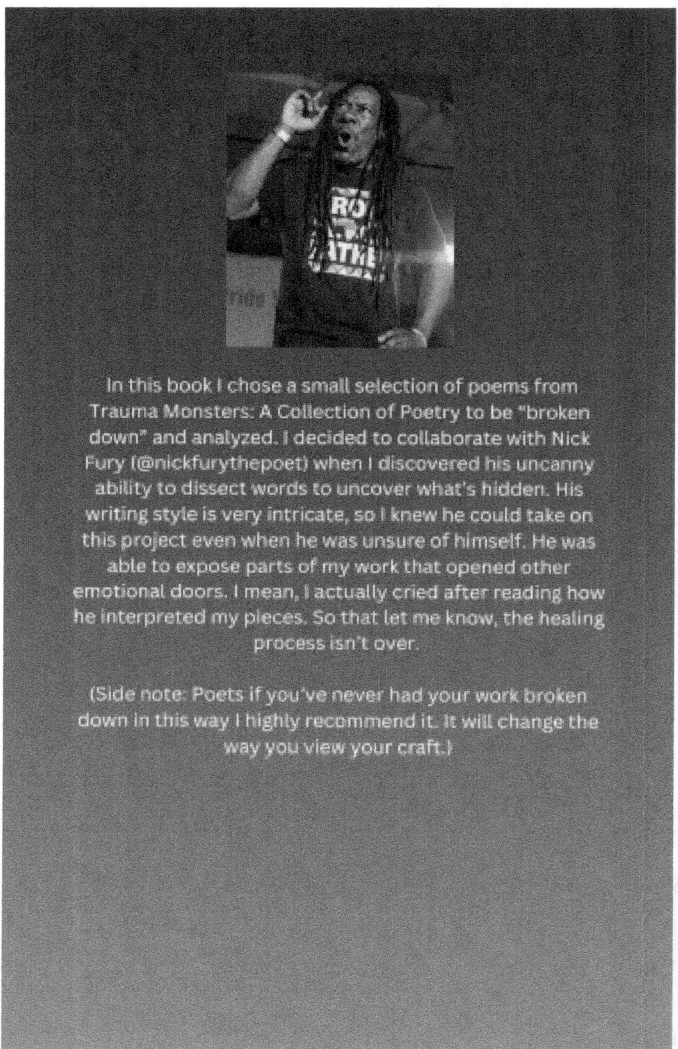

In this book I chose a small selection of poems from Trauma Monsters: A Collection of Poetry to be "broken down" and analyzed. I decided to collaborate with Nick Fury (@nickfurythepoet) when I discovered his uncanny ability to dissect words to uncover what's hidden. His writing style is very intricate, so I knew he could take on this project even when he was unsure of himself. He was able to expose parts of my work that opened other emotional doors. I mean, I actually cried after reading how he interpreted my pieces. So that let me know, the healing process isn't over.

(Side note: Poets if you've never had your work broken down in this way I highly recommend it. It will change the way you view your craft.)

Don't miss out!

Visit the website below and you can sign up to receive emails whenever JonKeL publishes a new book. There's no charge and no obligation.

https://books2read.com/r/B-A-HWHX-ZEEYC

BOOKS 2 READ

Connecting independent readers to independent writers.

Did you love *Trauma Monsters: The Breakdowns*? Then you should read *Trauma Monsters: A Collection of Poetry*[1] by JonKeL!

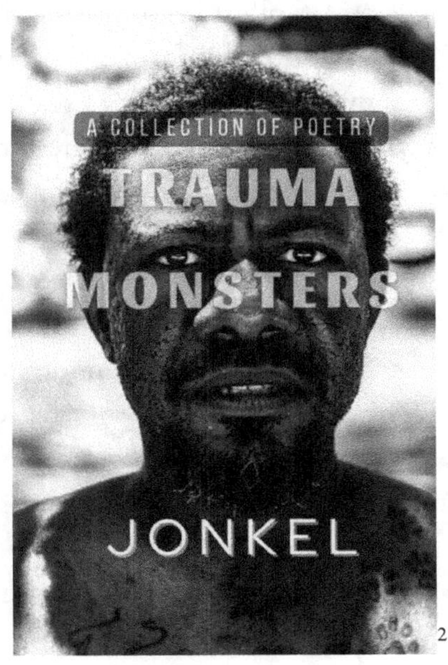

[2]

(Eccentrich @Be.Eccentrich.Inc) "When Jon told me he was writing a book, I knew it would be filled with incredible poems that told amazing stories about a tough childhood deserving of redemption, so I was excited to read it."

(Jacob Mayberry @BlackChakra88) "Everyday I gain more respect for JonKeL. He's someone that's worked for his national ranking. He's someone that consistently works for how good he is in poetry."

(Nick Fury @NickFuryThePoet) "Since JonKeL has been mentoring me, I've grown as an artist significantly. He provided a space for me to share, give me feedback that was more nuanced, and challenged me to

---

1. https://books2read.com/u/4Noz5J

2. https://books2read.com/u/4Noz5J

explore my vulnerabilities through my writing. He always encourages me to find my most authentic voice."

The author invites readers to enter his world through powerful poetry. Trauma Monsters: A Collection of Poetry contains 23 dynamic poems that also includes additional information about each piece. This will provide more insight on the author's creative process and the monsters he's been trying to put to rest. We are often haunted by our past traumas, and sometimes the healthiest coping comes in the form of poetic expression.

Jonathan David Kelly, better known as JonKeL, is a South Florida actor, writer, and creative director. His artistic journey began as a child, winning essay and poetry contests in grade school. Inspired by his father who was also a poet, he connected with this genre of writing for its healing properties, after journaling turned into therapy. It became the healthy, creative outlet he needed to deal with life's struggles. Writing about subjects most youth are too young to process, like domestic violence and drug abuse, creative expression was his first remedy for dealing with the pain.